Howdy! Hola! Bonjour! Guten Tag!

I'm a *very special book*. You see, I'm traveling around the world making new friends. I hope I've met another friend in you. Please go to

www.BookCrossing.com

and enter my BCID number (shown below). You'll discover where I've been and who has read me, and can let them know I'm safe here in your hands. Then... *READ and RELEASE me!*

BCID: 425-15735252

MONSTERS

PHOENIX

BY BONNIE JUETTNER

KIDHAVEN PRESS
A part of Gale, Cengage Learning

GALE
CENGAGE Learning™

Detroit • New York • San Francisco • New Haven, Conn • Waterville, Maine • London

LIBRARY OF CONGRESS CATALOGING-IN-PUBLICATION DATA

Juettner, Bonnie.
  Phoenix / by Bonnie Juettner.
     p. cm. — (Monsters)
  Includes bibliographical references and index.
  ISBN 978-0-7377-4045-5 (hardcover)
  1. Phoenix (Mythical bird) I. Title.
  GR830.P4J84 2008
  398'.469—dc22

                                                            2008029778

KidHaven Press
27500 Drake Rd.
Farmington Hills, MI 48331

ISBN-13: 978-0-7377-4045-5
ISBN-10: 0-7377-4045-0

Printed in the United States of America
1 2 3 4 5 6 7 12 11 10 09 08

CONTENTS

Chapter 1

Rising from the Ashes

Do not expect ever to see a phoenix. They are very rare. According to ancient myths, only one phoenix may live on Earth at one time. This one phoenix lives in a peaceful, secluded place—maybe even in the original **Garden of Eden**. It lives out a long life there. Some sources say that it lives for 500 years. Other stories say that the phoenix always lives for 1,000 or more years. When it grows old, it flies to the city of Heliopolis, in Egypt. It builds itself a nest out of pleasant-smelling twigs and spices, such as cinnamon, frank-incense, and myrrh.

When the nest is ready, the phoenix lights it on fire. Ancient authors were not sure how the phoenix manages to do this. Some sources say it rubs two sticks together to generate a spark. Then it beats its wings to fan the flames, providing the fire with oxygen. In the flaming nest, the phoenix burns itself alive.

THE NEXT PHOENIX

If any other animal were burned to death, that would be the end of the story. Not so with the phoenix. Out of the ashes of its nest, a new, young phoenix emerges. This young phoenix gathers myrrh and makes an egg out of it. Inside the egg, it places the remaining ashes from the fire that caused its predecessor's death. The young phoenix

An illustration from a 12th-century Latin natural history book shows a phoenix using its beak and talons to build a nest of twigs, only to set the nest on fire and lie in the flames, burning itself alive.

takes the ash-filled egg and flies with it to the temple of the sun god, Ra, in Heliopolis. It places the egg on the sun god's altar. Then it flies away to a remote location and is not seen again for another 500 or 1,000 years.

In an entranceway in the tomb of Peshedu, an Egyptian worker from the late 14th-century B.C. is overseen by a large, phoenixlike bird figure. The oldest stories about the phoenix originated in ancient Egypt.

The phoenix is not a real animal, of course. It lives only in myths, legends, and stories of fantastic creatures. But many ancient scholars thought the phoenix was real. The oldest stories of the phoenix come from Egypt. Egypt also has an older story about the phoenix. In this story, the phoenix does not go up in flames. Instead, it builds a **chrysalis**. Although the phoenix is a myth, there are real animals that can build a chrysalis, which is a covering to protect the animal as it transforms itself from one life stage to another. A caterpillar builds one when it is going to become a butterfly. (People sometimes confuse the chrysalis of a butterfly with the cocoon of a moth.) Inside its chrysalis, the phoenix dies. Then a worm crawls out of the phoenix's rotting corpse. The worm grows into a new phoenix. It is just like the phoenix that died, except for one thing: It is the opposite sex. A dying male phoenix produces a worm that will grow into a female phoenix—and vice versa.

Many ancient Greeks and Romans visited Egypt. They learned about the phoenix. Then Greek and Roman storytellers began to tell new stories about this fantastic bird. The Greeks told a story in which the phoenix bathes every day in a cool well. As it bathes, it sings songs of praise to the sun god. (For the Greeks, the sun god was Apollo.) Every day, Apollo's horses would pull his chariot containing the sun across the sky. But for a short time, the chariot would stop over the phoenix's well so Apollo could listen to the song of the phoenix.

ETERNAL LIFE

Many early Christian scholars believed the stories about the phoenix. They used the story of the phoenix to prove that it was possible for Jesus to rise from the dead. One scholar, Tertullian, wrote that God would not deny Jesus the same act—rising from the dead—that he allowed an Arabian bird to do. Some Christians were skeptical, though. Saint Augustine wrote that phoenix stories were nothing more than a childish **fantasy**.

Jewish scholars were fascinated by the phoenix's ability to live forever. According to one Jewish story, the phoenix was one of the animals living in the Garden of Eden. God told Adam and Eve that they could eat any fruit in the garden, except the fruit of the tree of the knowledge of good and evil. But Eve ate the fruit from the tree, offered it to Adam, and offered it as well to all the other animals in the garden. The phoenix was the only animal to refuse—so it was the only animal God allowed to remain in the Garden of Eden. Adam, Eve, and all the other animals were banished. Nothing ever dies in the Garden of Eden—so the phoenix must fly out of Eden when it is ready to die.

Christian lore supports the idea that the phoenix lives in the Garden of Eden. One early Christian author, Lactantius, wrote that the phoenix lived in a

An illustration depicts a phoenix rising from its ashes, a symbol of eternal life that is found in both Christian and Jewish lore.

wooded grove. In the phoenix's home, there were no diseases, no old age, no death, no crime, no greed, no anger, no violence, no grief, no hunger, and no bad weather. At sunrise, the phoenix would plunge its body into a stream of water. Then, flying to the top of a tree, it would begin to sing so sweetly that no other animal could imitate its voice.

In some stories, though, the phoenix does leave its garden. One Jewish story says that the phoenix was on the **ark** with Noah. Noah was having a hard time coming up with food for all of the animals. When he came to the phoenix, he asked it if it was hungry. It was, but, seeing how busy and frustrated Noah was, the phoenix chose not to eat. It said to Noah, "I saw that thou wast busy, so I said to myself, I will give thee no trouble."[1] As a reward, God granted the phoenix the ability to live forever.

Russia's Firebird

Phoenix stories traveled north from Greece and Rome to eastern Europe. Then the stories made their way east, to Russia. Russian myths refer to the phoenix as the **firebird** (for obvious reasons). In many of these stories, a czar, or king, discovers that fruit is being stolen from his orchard. The czar has three sons, each of whom takes a turn staying in the orchard all night to observe the thief. The first two sons fall asleep and miss their chance. The third stays awake and manages to take a feather from the firebird, who has been stealing the fruit. The story varies, but usually ends with the third son making his fortune, marrying a princess, and becoming the owner of the firebird.

A Real Bird?

Could the phoenix have been real? Scholars think the stories of the Egyptian phoenix may have been inspired by the flamingo of east Africa. This flamingo nests on salt flats where it is too hot for eggs or chicks to survive. To cool the nests, the flamingo builds a mound several inches tall. The air inside the nest is slightly cooler than the air on

A Russian myth tells the story of the phoenixlike firebird, which is discovered in an orchard by the czar's son, who manages to pluck one of its feathers.

the flats. As hot air rises from the flats around the nests, it produces an optical illusion, making it seem as though the nest is on fire.

Other scholars, however, think that the story began when a heron nested at the temple in Heliopolis. Eventually the nest was deserted, but occasionally

The bird of paradise, with its long, bright tail, is one of several exotic birds that may have inspired stories about the phoenix.

another heron would come to nest there. At one time, too, New Guinea's bird of paradise, which is a real bird, was thought to be a phoenix. Some scholars have also speculated that phoenix stories might have been based on the golden eagle. No matter where the phoenix story began, however, it traveled around the globe, flying to Saudi Arabia, Russia, and eventually the Far East—China and Japan.

CHAPTER 2

IMMORTAL BIRD

hinese mythology tells us of a bird with fiery feathers. Its tail feathers are in China's five sacred colors: red, blue, yellow, white, and black. It has Chinese characters written on all the parts of its body. On its head is written the character for excellence. Its wing reads "duty," its back "good manners," its abdomen "belief," and its chest "mercy." This bird is called the **fenghuang** in China, and the **fusicho**, or **immortal** bird, in Japan.

In China the fenghuang is considered to be two animals. In some stories it is one bird with two heads. The feng was the male bird and stood for the Sun and summer. The huang was the female bird and stood for the cycles of the moon. The huang was also the symbol of the Chinese empress.

(The male emperor was not represented by the feng, but by the dragon.) The feng and huang also stood for two kinds of energy, yang and yin. In Chinese medicine, yang energy is hot and aggressive, while yin energy is cool and flowing.

One variation on the phoenix is the Japanese Ho-Wo bird, a beast with male and female versions that appear only on special occasions, such as the birth of an emperor, much like the Chinese fenghuang.

The Chinese version of the phoenix, a colorful bird known as the fenghuang, is said to appear only during times of peace and prosperity.

16　Phoenix

Some scholars say the fenghuang is actually made of parts of many different animals. They say it has the breast of a goose, the hindquarters of a stag, the neck of a snake, the tail of a fish, the forehead of a fowl, the down of a duck, the marks of a dragon, the back of a tortoise, the face of a swallow, and the beak of a cock. It is said to be 9 feet (2.7m) tall.

Is It a Phoenix?

Is the fenghuang a phoenix? Many scholars say it cannot be. They point out that the fenghuang does not burn itself up and rise from its own ashes. But other scholars feel that rising from its ashes is not important. They point out that the fenghuang, with its large size and fiery feathers, looks exactly like a phoenix.

In addition, the fenghuang, like the phoenix, nests far away from people, in a secluded place. It sings beautifully. It also loves human music. It was believed that if one sat and played music under a wu t'ung tree, the fenghuang might appear and bless the musician by singing along. But most importantly of all, the fenghuang, like the phoenix, is immortal. It can live forever.

Harbinger of Peace

The Chinese fenghuang is as rare an animal as the Western phoenix. It appears only occasionally. In fact, it appears as rarely as another Chinese animal —the unicorn. In China both fenghuang and unicorn are known for appearing only during times of peace and prosperity. In ancient times, if someone saw a fenghuang, the sighting would be reported to the emperor right away. It would be considered a sign of peace to come.

It is said that the fenghuang first appeared in China in around 2600 B.C. At the time the emperor was Huangdi, China's Yellow Emperor. A time of peace and prosperity followed the sighting of the fenghuang. During Huangdi's reign, writing was invented. Huangdi's wife, the empress, invented a method for harvesting silk from silkworms and weaving the silk into cloth. According to some stories, Huangdi himself became an immortal, like the fenghuang, when he died.

The Tree Without Evil

Closer to its Egyptian cousin lives the Persian phoenix. Persia is the area that, in biblical times, was called Mesopotamia. Today it makes up the countries of Iraq and Iran.

The Iranian phoenix is called the **simorg**. Like the phoenix and the fenghuang, the simorg is considered to be the king of the birds. It lives in a place that sounds much like the Garden of Eden. It builds its nest in a tree known as "the tree without evil and of many seeds." When the simorg flies away from the tree 1,000 shoots grow out of the tree. When it lands the shoots break and drop many seeds.

In a scene from an ancient Iranian tale, a phoenix-like bird called the simorg rescues an abandoned child named Zal and takes him to her nest.

In Iranian mythology the simorg rescues a child, Zal. First, Zal is abandoned in the mountains. The simorg rescues him and puts him in her nest with her own young. (Unlike the phoenix, there may be more than one simorg at a time.) Eventually Zal's father comes for him. The simorg gives Zal a feather to take with him. If he ever needs her, he can burn the feather to call her for help.

Later, Zal does call the simorg for help, as his son is being born. She helps Zal's wife through the birth. She also helps Zal's wife to recover after the birth. Many years later she heals the son and his horse when they are wounded by arrows.

Kurdish and Armenian folktales tell a similar story. In the Kurdish story the bird is called a **simir**. A hero rescues the simir's children from snakes. She gives him three feathers that he can use to call for help. In one story she carries the hero out of the **underworld**. (In many myths, people who die go to live in the underworld. They can enter it but cannot normally leave it again.) In the Armenian version of this story, the hero must feed the bird ("**sinam**" in Armenian) with sheep's fat and wine as she flies. When he runs out of sheep's fat, he cuts a chunk from his own leg to offer her. Knowing it is human flesh, she refuses. At the end of the journey, she heals his leg wound.

THE SIMORG'S EVIL TWIN

The simorg has an evil counterpart, the **kamak**. It lives on a mountaintop and looks like a black cloud. It spreads its wings across the world, so that the rain falls on its wings instead of on Earth. Then the Earth goes into a drought, and the kamak devours the starving people and animals. It can easily carry off panthers, crocodiles, and elephants. Eventually it is killed by the hero Esfandiar. In Armenian stories, the simorg's counterpart is the griffin.

As described in the classic tale of One Thousand and One Arabian Nights, *Sinbad the sailor escapes from the nest of a bird known as the roc by tying his turban to its leg and letting the bird carry him away in flight.*

An illustration from a 17th-century Persian text depicts the mythical simorg, which some scholars think may have been inspired not by a real bird, but by a bat.

Another classic story, *One Thousand and One Arabian Nights*, also includes a bird that could be the evil twin of the simorg. This bird is called the **roc**. Like the kamak, it happily picks up elephants in its claws and drops them onto rocks to kill them. The roc also drops large stones onto ships at sea, wrecking them. In *One Thousand and One Arabian Nights*, the sailor Sinbad is stranded in a roc's nest. He unties his turban and reties it to the bird's leg. Then Sinbad is carried away when the roc flies off. At first it flies so high that Sinbad can no longer see the Earth. But eventually it flies low enough for him to drop onto an island. Sinbad was lucky—the roc never lands anywhere on Earth, except in its nest.

The Real Simorg?

Just as scholars think the phoenix was inspired by a real bird, they also think that the idea for the simorg came from a real animal. Some think that the first simorg was a bat, because it scatters seeds. The fruit bats of southern Iran eat fruits and then spit out the seeds.

Scholars argue about the phoenix, the fenghuang, the simorg, and all the other variations of this bird. Could they all be one and the same? Some think all the giant birds in mythologies from around the world originally came from one source. Wherever the stories came from, the phoenix is with us to stay. Modern storytellers are fascinated by it—and have added new fantastic variations to phoenix lore.

CHAPTER 3

THE FIREBIRD

Prince Ivan is trapped in the realm of an evil giant, Kashchei. Kashchei is immortal. He cannot be killed. He is greatly feared, because he imprisons women and changes men to stone. Ivan, however, does not know any of this. He does not realize the danger he is in. In Kashchei's garden, Ivan meets the firebird. He steals a feather and runs away. Later, Ivan meets thirteen maidens and falls in love with one. But they are Kashchei's prisoners.

Kashchei's servants catch sight of Ivan. They capture him and are about to turn him to stone. Suddenly, he waves his feather and the firebird appears. The firebird tells Ivan that Kashchei cannot be killed because he keeps his spirit in an egg. Ivan breaks the egg, and the monster dies. The prisoners

Costumed dancers depict the story of the firebird in a performance of the ballet of the same name, which was written by Russian composer Igor Stravinsky in 1909.

are instantly freed, and Ivan marries the maiden, who turns out to be a princess.

This might sound like the plot for a novel or a movie, but it is a ballet. It was written by Igor Stravinsky in 1909. Ballets Russes had hired Stravinsky to compose a ballet for its 1910 season. Stravinsky was fascinated by the story of the firebird, and he decided to compose music for it. Does the idea of using a feather to summon help sound familiar? Like the Iranian simorg, the Russian firebird can be called by someone who has one of its feathers.

The Firebird

A Human Phoenix

Stravinsky was not the only modern thinker to be enthralled by the phoenix. Philosopher Friedrich Nietzsche and writer D.H. Lawrence both admired phoenixes. They also looked at phoenixes in a new way. They thought that any person who was strong and brave enough to be willing to really change could be a kind of phoenix. They argued that a person, like the phoenix, could leave behind everything that had been a part of his or her life. (They did not expect humans to burn themselves alive. They only meant that people could set aside their most cherished ideas, habits, and plans.) Then, they proposed, that person could actually become somebody new.

Nietzsche and Lawrence both hoped to be that kind of person—the kind of person who could be like a phoenix. Nietzsche sometimes signed his work with the word *phoenix*. Lawrence adopted the phoenix as his personal symbol. Today, a plaster phoenix stands over his ashes at his tomb in Taos, New Mexico.

The Cherokee Phoenix

Even before Nietzsche and Lawrence began thinking about the phoenix, the Cherokee began to think along the same lines. They began to publish a newspaper called the *Cherokee Phoenix* in 1828. The paper was published in English and in the Cherokee language, using Cherokee symbols invented only a few

The *Cherokee Phoenix, which was published from 1828 to 1834, was created in part to empower Native Americans to rise up against the oppression of the United States government.*

years earlier by Sequoyah. The paper was intended to encourage Native American tribes to rise again, like a phoenix from its ashes.

Instead, the *Cherokee Phoenix* itself had to rise from its own ashes. In 1834 the paper ran out of money. Its supporters planned to reopen the paper. But the *Cherokee Phoenix* had made many enemies. Its editors had spoken out against the Indian Removal Act. (The Indian Removal Act was the law Congress passed authorizing the removal of the

Cherokee, and other Native Americans, from their native lands.) Enemies of the *Phoenix* raided its offices. They took printing type out of the office and stamped it into the dirt outside. They stole the printing press, and they set the building on fire. A few years later, the Cherokee were forced to march on the Trail of Tears to Oklahoma.

Many years afterward, though, the *Cherokee Phoenix* rose from its own ashes. It is published today in Tahlequah, Oklahoma.

THE ORDER OF THE PHOENIX

Like the *Cherokee Phoenix*, the phoenix of ancient myths has risen from its ashes to appear in stories written by modern authors. When a story from ancient times contains fantastic creatures, such as a phoenix, it is called a myth. But when writers today compose stories that include impossible animals,

Harry Potter is assisted in his battle with a basilisk monster by a phoenix named Fawkes in both the print and big-screen versions of J.K. Rowling's Harry Potter and the Chamber of Secrets.

these stories are called fantasy. (If the stories are based on speculation about technological advances that science might make possible, they are called **science fiction**.)

The most famous phoenix in a fantasy novel today is probably Fawkes, the phoenix who saves Harry Potter in J.K. Rowling's *Harry Potter and the Chamber of Secrets*. Harry first sees Fawkes in the office of Albus Dumbledore, the headmaster for Hogwarts School of Witchcraft and Wizardry. But he does not realize Fawkes is a phoenix. Dumbledore steps out of the room for a moment, and Fawkes suddenly bursts into flames, burning down to ash. When Dumbledore returns, a shocked Harry tells him what happened. Dumbledore responds, "About time, too. . . . He's been looking dreadful for days; I've been telling him to get a move on."[2]

Later in the same story, Harry must fight a **basilisk** monster in the Chamber of Secrets. Fawkes appears and helps him fight, but Harry is bitten. He knows the poison in the basilisk's fang will kill him. But he does not realize that phoenix tears have the ability to heal wounds. Fawkes weeps over Harry, and he is healed.

The Phoenix and Its Egg

Long before J.K. Rowling was born, Edith Nesbit was writing fantasy stories for children. In 1904 she published *The Phoenix and the Carpet*. In this book four children decide to test some fireworks in their bedroom. It is not safe to set off fireworks indoors because they can cause fires. In this case, the children's bedroom carpet catches fire. The carpet is ruined. The children's parents buy a new carpet. When the carpet is unrolled in the bedroom, the children discover an egg.

Several days later, the egg falls into the fireplace and hatches. A phoenix emerges. One child tries to touch it, and the phoenix responds, "Be careful; I am not nearly cool yet." The phoenix tells the children his story. It turns out that the carpet in which the egg had been wrapped was a wishing carpet. The children could stand on the carpet and wish to be in another place, and it would take them. At first, they are about to be discovered out of bed at night. "Wish yourself there," advises the phoenix, "and then wish the carpet back in its place."[3] They do, and they land in their beds, just before their father arrives to check on them.

Since Nesbit and Rowling, many fantasy writers have included phoenixes in their work. In her Immortals series, Tamora Pierce has her heroine Daine visit the home of the Immortals, where sunbirds fly through the air and burst into flames every evening at sunset. Neil Gaiman wrote a short story, "Sunbird," in which members of an eating club run out of interesting foods to eat. They decide to capture and cook a phoenix, but when they eat it, all but one of them bursts into flames and dies. The remaining club member, who had been very old, becomes young again. In his blog, Gaiman once joked, "Making omelettes with the phoenix egg is not recommended. The resulting fires can cause problems, for a start."[4]

Lawrence Yep has written a whole series about a boy and a tiger who guard a fenghuang egg. The tiger, Mr. Hu, is a magician, and the boy, Tom, is his apprentice. At the beginning of Tom's apprenticeship, Mr. Hu explains that the fenghuang "has the gift to transform evil hearts into good ones."[5] Because the fenghuang was afraid its power might be misused—it might be reversed to force people to do evil things—it went back into its egg. Guardians were appointed to protect the fenghuang as it slept in its egg, to make sure that it was only awakened in a time of peace.

Writers have imagined phoenixes that could heal people's bodies and souls. But engineers have imagined phoenixes with many other kinds of gifts—phoenixes that could rebuild cities, fly like a jet but on the ground, help fight wars, and even travel to Mars.

Phoenix

CHAPTER 4

THE NEW PHOENIXES

On October 8, 1871, a fire began on Chicago's West Side. Within minutes, it was out of control. It kept going, consuming home after home, until it reached Lake Michigan. The fire destroyed one-third of the city, killed 300, and left 100,000 people homeless.

Thirty-five years later, another large city, San Francisco, was hit by an earthquake. The earthquake was devastating. But even worse were the fires it started. The earthquake had broken water pipes, so firefighters ran completely out of water after spraying the fire for five minutes. They had to pump fluid out of the sewers and water out of the bay. In the end most of the city lay in ruins, more than 3,000 people were dead, and more than half of the city's people were homeless.

Phoenix Cities

Chicago and San Francisco recovered from their fires. Today they are thriving metropolises. Because they were destroyed by fire and then recovered, Chicago and San Francisco are called phoenix cities. Oddly enough, the only U.S. city that was actually named after a phoenix was never destroyed by fire. Phoenix, Arizona, was named by its founder, Darrell Duppa. He remarked that, "a new city will spring phoenix-like upon the ruins of a former civilization."[6] Duppa meant that the city would rest on land that was once the home of an ancient civilization, the **Hohokam**.

A spiral was carved in rock by inhabitants of the ancient Hohokam civilization, which inhabited the area of what is now southern Arizona near the modern city of Phoenix throughout the first millennium A.D.

In 2005 some people began to hope that New Orleans, Louisiana, might become a phoenix city. New Orleans was hit by Hurricane Katrina in August 2005. The hurricane attacked the city with winds that swirled at 145 miles per hour (233kph). The winds went on for eight hours. The city survived the winds. But the next day levees standing between New Orleans and the water of Lake Pontchartrain broke, and water poured into the city. Eighty percent of New Orleans was submerged. In some places the water was 20 feet (6m) deep. Eventually the water receded. Some people decided to find other places to live. But others came back and began to rebuild. They hoped New Orleans, like the phoenix, could rise again.

THE CAR THAT LOOKED LIKE A JET

No driver would want his or her car to catch on fire. Strangely enough, though, several cars are named after the Russian firebird. So is at least one race course. In the 1950s General Motors made an experimental car called the XP-21 Firebird. It was meant to be a car that would look and drive like a jet. The XP-21 had a turbine engine, like a jet plane. It could go 100 miles per hour (161kph) easily. In fact, it could even go over 200 miles per hour (322kph). But at those speeds the tires flew off the car in test drives.

GM never released the experimental Firebird designs to the public. The first Firebird was dangerous,

The New Phoenixes

35

partly because its turbine engine was so strong. In one of the first test drives, engineer Charles McCuen was startled to find out how easily the car accelerated. It did not slow down when he took his foot off the accelerator. McCuen and Firebird I wound up sliding under the track's guardrail and rolling into the grass. The car was totaled, and McCuen's life was saved—barely—by the headrest built into the seat. Still, Firebird's design taught the company how to make a car's ride smoother. GM's engineers also learned new methods for improving a car's brakes. A car that can drive fast has to be able to stop fast, too.

THE PHOENIX AT WAR

The British and American militaries have designed their own phoenixes for use in wartime. The British phoenix was an **unmanned aerial vehicle (UAV)**. It could fly into dangerous areas alone, with no pilot. It was designed to do surveillance. This means it could take photos to send back to the troops. The photos could give the military important information about what was happening in other areas. Troops could control the phoenix from the ground, with a remote control. Or they could program it in advance to fly a certain route. It could land with the help of a parachute. The British phoenix was used in peacekeeping missions and in the Iraq war. But it was retired when the new Watchkeeper UAV was built.

An F-14 Tomcat fighter jet soars skyward carrying six AIM-54 Phoenix missiles, each of which could be launched at a different target.

The American military phoenix is a **missile**. It used to be the Navy's only long-range air-to-air missile. Called the AIM-54 Phoenix, it was carried in clusters of six by the F-14 Tomcat, a fighter jet. (The Navy has jet planes in its arsenal—they can take off and land on large ships called aircraft carriers.) The six Phoenix missiles carried by a Tomcat could be launched against six different targets, all at the same time.

The New Phoenixes

Each Phoenix missile cost the Navy $477,131. But they were fast and effective. They could travel faster than 3,000 miles per hour (4,800kph). And they could travel farther than 100 nautical miles (115 statute miles, or 184km).

The AIM-54 was retired a few years ago. But the military still has a few left. The National Aeronautics and Space Administration (NASA) is considering them for high-speed tests. Phoenix missiles can reach speeds up to Mach 5, enough to make them hypersonic. In other words, they can travel faster than the speed of sound. The Phoenix missiles could be used as test beds, which means each missile could carry a material that NASA wanted to learn about. First their explosive warheads would be removed. The guidance systems would be replaced with lighter systems. The missiles could carry new materials that are designed to protect aircraft from high temperatures. Then NASA could study the materials after the missile landed to see how they held up at high speeds.

THE MISSION TO MARS

NASA is also doing scientific research using another type of phoenix—the *Phoenix Mars Lander*. In 2008 NASA sent a mission to Mars. The mission was dubbed the Phoenix because it rose from the embers, or ashes, of previous missions to Mars. It also used some of the same equipment that was used on previous missions. For example, it used the

An artist's depiction shows NASA's Phoenix Mars Lander *touching down on the surface of the red planet. Launched in August 2007, the craft landed on Mars in May 2008.*

The New Phoenixes

lander from the 2001 Mars Surveyor mission. It also used scientific instruments from the *Mars Polar Lander.*

This time, the Phoenix Mars mission accomplished something NASA had not managed to do before. It confirmed that the circumpolar regions of Mars have frozen water under the topsoil. Scientists previously knew that there was ice there, but they thought the ice could have been some other frozen liquid. Phoenix's instruments confirmed that it was water. This was exciting news. It meant that it was even more likely that life in some form might once have existed on Mars.

One cannot expect to see a real, live phoenix in one's lifetime because this bird is a mythological beast. Imaginary or not, though, the phoenix will continue to inspire writers, artists, and engineers. It will continue flying to awesome heights and exploring new worlds. Where will the phoenix turn up next?

Notes

Chapter 1: Rising from the Ashes

1. Mary Francis Macdonald, "Phoenix Redivivus," *Phoenix*, Winter 1960, pp. 187–206.

Chapter 3: The Firebird

2. J.K. Rowling, *Harry Potter and the Chamber of Secrets*. New York: Scholastic, 1999, p. 207.
3. Edith Nesbit, *The Phoenix and the Carpet*, 1904. www.classicreader.com/read.php/bookid.422/sec.1/.
4. Neil Gaiman, Neil Gaiman's Journal, March 20, 2003. http://journal.neilgaiman.com/2003_03_01_archive.html.
5. Lawrence Yep, *The Tiger's Apprentice, Book I*. New York: HarperCollins, 2003, pp. 39–40.

Chapter 4: The New Phoenixes

6. Quoted in Encyclopedia Britannica Online, "Darrell Duppa," 2008. www.britannica.com/EBchecked/topic/174010/Darrell-Duppa.

GLOSSARY

ark: In the Judeo-Christian tradition, the boat built by Noah to hold pairs of Earth's animals. The ark was intended to preserve Earth's animal life during a flood.

basilisk: A mythological animal, shaped like a large snake, but with arms and legs. A basilisk's bite was supposed to be deadly.

chrysalis: The pupa stage of a butterfly's life cycle.

fantasy: A type of book or story that contains magic, imaginary creatures or other elements that would not normally be encountered in real life.

fenghuang: A mythological Chinese bird believed by some scholars to be a phoenix.

firebird: The Russian phoenix.

fusicho: The Japanese fenghuang.

Garden of Eden: In the Judeo-Christian tradition, the place where Adam and Eve lived until they disobeyed God.

Hohokam: An ancient Native American civilization from the American Southwest.

immortal: Able to live forever.

kamak: The simorg's evil twin.

missile: A long-range bomb.

roc: A phoenixlike bird from *One Thousand and One Arabian Nights*, much like the kamak.

science fiction: Stories based on speculation about technological advances that science might someday make possible.

simir: The Kurdish simorg.

simorg: A mythological Iranian bird, much like a phoenix.

sinam: The Armenian simorg.

underworld: A place where people in Greek and Roman myths go when they die.

unmanned aerial vehicle (UAV): A military vehicle that can fly and do surveillance without a pilot. It can be controlled by remote control or can be programmed to fly a particular route.

FOR FURTHER EXPLORATION

BOOKS

Marius Barbeau, *The Golden Phoenix and Other French Canadian Fairy Tales*. New York: Walck, 1963. Includes a long narrative of the French Canadian version of the Russian firebird story, along with other fairy tales.

Pauline Baynes, *Questionable Creatures: A Bestiary*. Grand Rapids, MI: Eerdmans, 2006. A beautifully illustrated dictionary of monsters, including the phoenix.

John Harris, *Greece! Rome! Monsters!* Los Angeles: J. Paul Getty Museum, 2002. An illustrated bestiary in dictionary form.

Margaret Mayo and Jane Ray, *Mythical Birds and Beasts from Many Lands*. London: Orchard, 1996. A collection of stories about mythical birds and animals, including the story of the Egyptian phoenix.

Joe Nigg, *Wonder Beasts: Tales and Lore of the Phoenix, the Griffin, the Unicorn, and the Dragon*. Englewood, CO: Libraries Unlimited, 1995. Includes little-known stories, legends, and myths about each animal.

Lisl Weil, *Of Witches and Monsters and Wondrous Creatures*. New York: Atheneum, 1985. An account of how stories about monsters develop. Includes the Egyptian phoenix and the Russian firebird.

Jane Yolen, *The Firebird*. HarperCollins, 2002. The story of *The Firebird* ballet.

Web Sites

The Aberdeen Bestiary, University of Aberdeen (www.abdn.ac.uk/bestiary/bestiary.hti). An online encyclopedia of beasts, searchable by animal. Includes translations of medieval texts and images from manuscripts.

Animals in the Middle Ages, the Medieval Bestiary (http://bestiary.ca/index.html). An encyclopedia of medieval references to real and mythological animals. Searchable by animal and by medieval manuscript.

Encyclopedia Mythica (www.pantheon.org). An online encyclopedia of mythology, folklore, and religion. Includes the mythologies of Africa, the Americas, and Asia as well as classical Greek and Roman mythology. In addition to stories about the phoenix itself, includes information about the human Phoenix, who Greek myths say was the tutor to Achilles.

***The Phoenix and the Carpet*, Classic Reader** (www.classicreader.com/booktoc.php/sid.3/bookid. 422). An online copy of Edith Nesbit's novel about children who discover and hatch a phoenix egg. The Web site includes many other classic texts and a search engine that can be used to search within the books—a useful tool for students who are writing reports in which they analyze themes and symbols.

INDEX

Picture Credits

About the Author

Bonnie Juettner is a writer and editor of children's reference books and educational videos. She loves fantasy stories and myths, especially when they contain phoenixes. Originally from McGrath, Alaska, she currently lives in Kenosha, Wisconsin.